Passing Through Humansville

Sundress Publications • Knoxville, TN

Editor: Erin Elizabeth Smith
Editorial Assistants: Laura Villareal and Anna Black

Special thanks to Lauren Haynes and Jenna Geisinger.

Colophon: This book is set in Gentium Basic.

Front Cover Design: Charli Barnes

Back Cover Design: Kristen Ton

Book Design: Erin Elizabeth Smith

Passing Through Humansville
Karen Craigo

Acknowledgements

It is with sincere appreciation that I acknowledge the editors of the magazines where some of these poems first appeared.

Connotation Press: "Ten Sources of Light"
diode: "Inventory"
Escape Into Life: "La Maison Française," "Cow Ridge," "Small Case
      Against Perfect Solitude," and "Field Trip."
Gather: "Advent" and "Meditation With Cat and Toddler"
Human, All Too Human: "The Art of Rhetoric"
MockingHeart Review: "Samhain"
One: "The Movement You Need"
Pencil Box Press: "Ten Sources of Light"
Shantih: "The Art of Rhetoric," "Family Photo Shoot," "For Brenna
      <3 Ernie," "Good Night in the Blanket Fort,"
      "Tasseomancy," and "The Toddler Is Overtired."
Terrain: "Passing Through Humansville"

Table of Contents

III.

For Copernicus and Keats, who live up to their names
and keep me tethered to humansville.

I.

Meditation With Cat and Toddler

And here I sit with a body reluctant
to bend, a brain that won't still, a cat
that bumps me for attention, and a toddler
who will come, who has punched
me in the eye for pure love. I'm not sure
how to start, but the cat knows. He suggests
compassion, to lie against the dear one,
and if she gets too still, to bite her hand
because there is no virtue in denying
your nature. You offer a constant rumble
of *om*. You are conscious of her breath,
of the small one who approaches,
then sits down silent by her side.

Before He Was Born, I Sang Night Songs

When I hear the soft constriction of throat,
so easy to miss, he's got it. There is something certain
in the latch, firm, parasitic, drawing the nectar
down. Those first days he lives on teaspoons and I
feel fuller, like I could feed anything that aches.
There is nothing on this sphere I won't pull to me,
won't sing to in the dark. Let's call this what it is—
the last moment I am everything, his sweetness
and his sound. He still vibrates with my humming.
Those lullabies I never knew the words to
chime past their making like a singing bowl.

On His Brother's Second Birthday

My son, eight, is inconsolable.
He says he misses the baby,
who won't be back, though
I remind him our younger selves
don't go away—they live on,
deeper and deeper within us.
I'm here to comfort, to suggest
his is a childish thought,
but I too mourn the baby,
the down of his hair, sweet milk
on his breath. We must believe
an infant resides in all of us.
Come. Sniff the hollow of my neck—
a scent so soft you're not
even certain it's there.

Spelling Test Friday

I won't let him go until he spells
PUGNACITY. It's on his list
with its cousins, PUGNACIOUS,
IMPUGN. And there's PUNISH,
no G, just to mess with him,
as English does, and it's doing
right now, as I spar with words
like a pugilist. It's no wonder
he works around them,
always in trouble for sketching
in class, heroes and monsters,
zombies and plants. And just now
I opened the notebook
I like to write in, and I found
this drawing, a champion
in a cape, pot-bellied, grinning,
with two legs but six
inexplicable knees.
BAD BEHAVIOR, my son
labeled it, and I know
he gets it, understand
he's going to do fine.

Avocado

The avocado cups a hand
around its pit. I read
that if you keep a core
in the guacamole,
it won't go brown. After
my second child, the doctor
pushed ligation. I was
grandmother-aged, holding
a baby to breast. This body,
though, is ripe, and you don't
want the fruit too firm—
it is best when it begins
to go soft. Month by month,
I drop my eggs, still
no sign of ceasing. In me
two sunflowers wind
toward their orbs.
But this is not a poem
about sunflowers. I'm trying
to say that deep inside
the nurturing flesh,
there is a still-firm core.

Tasseomancy

My toddler likes to share
my coffee. He picks up the cup
and drinks deeply, and I hear
his throat work, the smack
of lips. This morning
we're down to the dregs
and he pulls the cup away,
grounds speckling his lips.
We share a future, and maybe
we can read it in our mug.
To do it, you start at the rim
then peer lower to the base,
the far future. Flying things
are a good omen—a kite
and our wishes come true,
a bird in flight, good news.
For as long as we've drunk,
we've thirsted to know
what the future holds.
But there is much to be said
for the present as we stare
into the vessel, close enough
to smell the other's breath.

For Brenna <3 Ernie

Last night my son
drew a picture for Brenna,
who watches him sometimes
and is sweetness and joy.
They stand side by side
in blocky slacks, and you know
she's a girl by the bun
balanced like an apple
on her head. In the picture,
each wears a U for a smile
and they stand apart,
not touching nor able
to touch, their arms
short and handless.
When he gave it, he broke
into grief, racking sobs,
eyes closed in shame.
He loves her. Consider
his vision, two, standing,
so happy and plain
in their britches. It is
simple. There is nothing
easier; the beauty
hurts him, each one
dignified and glad,
small arms open
to possibility
in the twin flags
of their rectangle pants.

a student meeting the eligibility criteria
for emotional disturbance

—Public Schools Evaluation Report 5/12/14

concerns were noted
  parents
    have indicated
  classroom teacher
    charted

      depression and outbursts difficulty
      making friends stubbornly refuses and
       is fearful

         difficulty riding
     a bike, catching a ball
      and throwing

    picky eater
        will yell
    or slam his fist

    doesn't want to risk
    failure doesn't initiate

      avoidance/escape

picks up scissors using
appropriate right thumbs-up
scissor grasp

    echolalia odd
prosody to his speech

mother drank
about two cups of coffee a day
but did not partake in illicit drugs
during pregnancy

kissed a boy on the shoulder
in class   hard
on himself but will say
he is bored

observed sticking his tongue
inside the marker cap   made
noises during art class   climbed
on his desk   rear end
in the air   required
verbal prompts

      He announced, "I am going to build a time machine"
      He said, "I like your hair"

The Toddler Is Overtired

So bone-weary, all he can do
is hop up and down in his crib,
and sing out syllables, and pull
the cat's tail, and jump some more.

I've never been that tired, up
hours longer than he should be,
eyes red and fighting to stay open.
It's a tired that jangles, zaps
his nerves, like being so hungry
you don't feel hungry anymore.

But even the electric eel
has to sleep sometimes
in the mud of an Amazon stream.
All day he finds his way with bursts
of small charge, his electricity
making up for weak eyes, and even
when he tries to rest amid reeds,
always there's a hum in him.

Good Night in the Blanket Fort

A promise has me sleeping
in the blanket fort, quilts piled
on hardwood, pillows arranged
in columns. These walls
protect us from blue night;
the boy's whispers, mine, rise.
But noises from outside are keener:
sound like a footstep, sound
like someone breathing.
I want to be brave in here, he says,
but what I like is company.
And we are fearless that way,
as we send invisible smoke signals
up into the boundless canopy,
brave, so brave together.

Casting a Vote at Rountree Elementary

It always rains on Election Day.
I feel sure of this, just as I'm sure
of the candidate, earnest blue farmer
willing, in this red state, to try.
The machine says I'm the eleventh
to cast a ballot, and it's dark outside,
but not in the cafetorium
with its posters of apples and calls
for RESPECT, TOLERANCE, all those ways
we want our kids to live. That's
a tough enough sell, to say nothing
of EMPATHY for obstructionists,
polluters, people with contempt
for my body. I draw the line—
it's how we vote here: We fill in
the missing part of an arrow
that points to our choice,
so that right to left we make
a sort of connection.

La Maison Française

My son sees no point
in learning French, but I've labeled
everything, *le lit, le divan, le chat.*
It's not my favorite, either,
so many letters unpronounced
like lights left on all day
in a vacant room. My accent is *terrible.*
Nevertheless, *le miroir* is speckled
with *le dentifrice, la bouilliore* sings
like *l'oiseau* in *la cuisine.*
I tell him he might need this—
one day he could broker *la détente*
or order a nice *vin de France*
for someone *tres jolie.*
And maybe it's enough
just to spot *les histoires*
our own words lug along
like a portmanteau.
At the end of all this, he'll know
some nouns, and he'll pronounce them
like I do, poorly, with a *soupçon*
of defiance at all that is wasted,
all that is left unsaid.

Field Trip

Today the butterfly house
releases monarchs, tags affixed
like tiny suitcases for their flight
south. I'm here to keep everyone
together, to make sure the bus leaves
no lighter than when it came.
One of the children has stolen the wing
of a sulfur. It was dead anyway,
so she palmed it, and now,
fingers flaked in gold, she tries
to work off its color.
A docent points out
a mourning cloak, faded and ripped,
three weeks old and probably
still laying eggs. She keeps going
till she dies, he tells me,
and at forty-five, with a baby,
I relate. Certain fall days
the sun can surprise us
with its insistence, can pin us
to the chair, and we picture
those migrating butterflies,
gold, gold, gold, gold,
gone.

Samhain

It's the night when the veil is thinnest—
this world, the other, rustle the same curtain
with their breath. The veil between having
and not having Milk Duds is barely present,
only three to a box. Apples are deadly,
and home-baked cookies, too, the veil
between grandma and sociopath
ripped wide. In ancient times, villagers
would place food beyond town's edge
to lead spirits away. They wore masks
to fool their ghosts. Tonight, the veil
between costume and none is stretched
by cold. Princesses wear tuques for tiaras.
Batmen are puffy with down.
You swore you'd be the one
who offered full-sized Snickers,
but look at you now,
bowl of Dum-Dums
by your door.

On Nov. 3, I Eyeball the Pumpkin

We did what was required.
Our zombie horde stumbled
down the avenue, faces
greened, clothes tattered.
The candy passed inspection,
all the good stuff claimed,
but on the table, the pumpkin
my son chose, the right shape
for apple-cheeked grin,
great circles of boo.
Turned one way it stares
at the sky, the other it stoops
in despair. All Saints, All Souls
are behind us, but the gourd
remains intact. *When
will we carve the pumpkin*,
my son asks, and we may yet.
Like so many things, this one
could go either way.

II.

Passing Through Humansville

Twice today, I'll slip into and out
of Humansville, both coming and going,
but now tendrils of fog span the road,

the layer of white like an old lady's hair
spread out behind her in rapture. Why not?
The oldest vessel can still hold

a drink, or else we'd call it a shard.
From his potter's wheel, my friend
can see sometimes a woman, old,

who bikes in looping circles
in the empty funeral lot,
insisting on the cursive of her name.

And maybe I've stepped on the ground
where my ashes will light.
Maybe, unknowing, I've danced.

Scab Sisters

That day we gathered in the wood, friends
and friends of friends, standing in a circle, earnest
about forging a bond with just a drop of our blood,
none of us equipped with a knife, all of us relieved.
That's how we became scab sisters—I picked a circle
from my ankle bone, a blister gone raw, just starting
to heal. Another scratched at her knee, and another
worked a cuticle or newly pierced ear, and then
we put it all together, what blood we could coax
or what damp pain. Someone might have said
something, but no one did—we just stood there,
under the trees, where once we had smuggled beer
and opened it and tasted, and it was terrible
and we were sure we were drunk—dared not finish
the other half of the can—but this thing was different,
it was holy, we were dryads rejoining the wood,
we were bound, or maybe we were only girls touching,
but it's been forty years and sometimes I stand
at the window, I look for them, arm in arm, cresting the hill,
fierce Horae shading my door, saying, *Come sister,*
we have need of you, and I come, of course, I come.

No Room

It's wrong to make this
about me. There was a baby,
born to be a bauble
on a tree, and we wait
for him, stick a candle
in each window, pop
a door in the calendar
to eat a square of candy.
But I'm sad and my bones
jingle, and the one
in the story I relate to
is that innkeeper,
full up, everyone
waiting for supper,
and here comes
this pregnant girl
on the back of an ass,
almost ready to pop. Damn,
but a hard day's work
should earn us a little rest,
not crisis after crisis,
fools who neglect to call
ahead. But the smallest
are due mercy, and he
pictures a tiny starfish hand
reaching in supplication
or blessing, and goddamn
that star is putting
down some light.

Advent

Sometimes I think about Joseph,
mere extra in the crèche, but how
he married the girl, all belly
and obedience, and had he not
it would have been a quick story,
"Pregnant Teen Stoned," hardly
a story at all—or at least not one
for the ages. He must have seen
the cresting head, second-
guessed all that had brought him
to the stable, but then he caught
the slippery savior, figured out
the rest, Mary offering what she knew
from the births she had witnessed,
barn animals giving testament
that they too emerged from a cave
into the dry world, it can happen.
I'd say Joseph alone deserves
a tree, branches bent nearly double
under the weight of all that light.

Small Case Against Perfect Solitude

Sometimes I listen for
that inner lake whose ripples
come and come.
When there is nothing
I feel empty but not
in the desired way, empty-
but-waiting-to-be-
filled—just alone, maybe
a little hungry.
And what words arrive
are jarring, like a sneeze
between movements,
a ringtone in a basilica.
I prefer the murmur
of voices in the west gallery,
furnace hum, a sketcher
dropping a pencil,
that paradiddle as it rolls
across the tile.

When We Find a Hurt Mouse

The man I love is kind enough
to bear the injured to the yard,
then with one stomp save it
from hours of suffering. Safe
to say, not all gentleness
is conveyed in a caress.
But just now I watch him
stroke the patchwork squares
of the giraffe's neck, receive
a blue tongue the length
of his arm, offer it a bit
of grain. The gift is raised
and pulled away, great head
lowering. The man touches
the reticulated neck, camouflage,
I know, but against what backdrop
might she hide? She is so exposed,
lacks even the means to call.

What Springs From the Ground

For affliction does not come from the dust, nor does trouble spring from the ground; yet man is born of trouble, as the sparks fly upward.
—Job 5:6-7

To be human, or to be any
good at it, you have to study
the rain: how each fat drop
slaps the wooden stairs just
like a mad palm, and together
the drops explain the sound
of one hand clapping.
We will be tested on this,
will be forced to describe
with exactitude the destruction
of the drop, how it hits
then springs up in shattered
hallelujahs. *The sparks
fly upward.* It says that in Job.
Our hero, a fool, never forsakes
the one who has forsaken,
who makes sport of him.
*Affliction does not come
from the dust,* it says,
but I'd prefer to think
it does, that the one we seek
for comfort doesn't rain
down our ruin for fun. Man
is born of trouble, but I
am a woman and between
my flinty thighs can make
some trouble of my own.
When it rains in the mountains
sometimes a gulley begins,

a fault, and eventually
the whole hill gives way.

Mary of Bethany

In church today a woman
rubbed the bald spot of the man
she loved, and did it all the way
through the message, the offering
and meditation. I know.
I opened my eyes to check.
And isn't that God, touching us
where we're most exposed,
loving even our emptiness,
those places soft with down.

Cow Ridge

Return is inevitable,
so the lead cow draws
a heavy line home.
On the ridge
they are backlit, they cast
blue shadows, their bodies
umber and red, like
the insides of your lids
when you press them
with a thumb.
Their path defines the break
between night and day
and from here it is
illuminated, a wash
of milk.

Evenings they descend
in perfect glory,
heads down, steps
measured. Is this
how we know we're not
wild? We spend days
eating clover like it's our job
until something in us
is iron and wants the magnet
home. It's solstice and the sky
will be pale for hours, long
after these sisters lie down
in their rows, long after
horses start to dream
on the hoof.

After the Blah Moon

A friend says the moon was nothing special
last night—full but ordinary, not
especially close. He'd seen better—moons
sized to crush a town, and in every
astonishing hue: pumpkin, Red Delicious,
a bare suggestion of corn. There is no magic
in a white moon, hanging over wheat stubble
like a bulb. Indigenous people called it
the Beaver Moon, the almanac says—time
to set the traps—but I am skeptical.
You can trap a beaver any time of year,
yet we picture a man pulled from his bed,
fumbling with rope on a tree-lined bank
where the moon is next to useless.
Trapping is nothing like harvest,
which works the farmers late into night
to beat the frost. Last night's moon
deserved an honest name—Spotlight Moon,
Moon That Resembles No Fruit, Moon
That Won't Let You Lose Your Way
Though You Walk in the Cold for Hours
and Try Like Hell, Moon That Makes
Shadow Puppets of Trees, That Figures
You Can Sleep Some Other Night, Moon
Whose Lunar Fingers Rake Your Face.
But friend, the moon hasn't changed.
It never really does, until we tromp on it,
our footsteps still fresh, decade after decade.
Take it up with the Earth, your rue,
your want of color, if you dare, that is—
if you would ask of her one more thing.

Ten Sources of Light

A century

1.

When you drive at
night you sometimes
see a glow that is a
town—everyone not
sleeping finds a circle
of light to read or sigh
by. In my town, there
is a hill that overlooks
its four avenues. I'd sit
there at night, choose
a particular light and
imagine the story
beneath: someone
cutting a body from a
photograph, someone
biting directly into a
hot loaf of bread. Two
make love. One
compares a palm to an
outline on a face. No
one is joyous by
lamplight, but some
find a quiet that is
happy or at least
content.

2.

There was a curve just
past the one-lane
bridge, but we opted
not to take it, so the
boy's car slid sideways
across a lawn. A better
poet would know the
type of tree that caved
in her door, but this
one remembers two
things: there was a
tree where I'd been
sitting, and the car was
not on fire—it was only
the light from the
dashboard glowing red
after I'd scrambled
into the lap of the boy.
The last thing I'd said
was that I wasn't
scared, and I'm still
not. I've always had a
fondness for trees.

3.

For Jenny Holzer.

A great artist came
from my hometown
and created this
moment when art
could be words
crossing a sign. She'd
say things like IN A
DREAM YOU SAW A WAY TO
SURVIVE AND YOU WERE
FULL OF JOY or PROTECT ME
FROM WHAT I WANT. I see
her installations from
time to time in
museums and I know
she walked the
hallways of my school.
Maybe we shared a
locker, maybe I read
from her book. What
we share now is the
idea that words can
possibly save us, so we
light them up, set
them marching.

4.

The day the eclipse
came I watched it
through a welder's
mask: dark stain
smothering the light. I
was a reporter in a
small town and the sun
was my beat. I walked
around the square,
seeking opinions—
what do you think of
the sun, I asked, and
have you ever seen
anything like this? I
could have
interviewed the birds
—suddenly quiet in the
middle of the day, it
seemed they had an
opinion. No one dares
to posit the tough
questions—where is
your god now, good
man, and do you really
believe your star will
come back?

5.

Already there's a
problem. My baby lies
in the blue glow of the
jaundice lamp, his
body not used to dry
air, so much room to
stretch and move. Yet
he is still. Little chest
rises and falls, left
hand curls into a fist. A
mask obscures his eyes
and we both think how
different this world is
from the one we were
expecting—the one
with rocking chairs
and soft singing, with
bright eyes making
sense of my blurred
face. You, little loaf,
are almost risen. How
warm you'll feel
against me. I can't wait
to breathe you in.

6.

Once I saw it in Ohio—
aurora, green gauze
rippling over stars. I
pulled over as we do
when something we
took to be black
gestures at us in color.
I know there are places
where these curtains
of light are
commonplace, and
maybe no one looks up
to regard them. But
where I parked, future
site of a shopping mall,
mounds of earth
growing soft in the
weather—that was a
place where the sky
stays put, where there
is so little to see that
we keep our eyes fixed
on the lines down the
middle of the road.

7.

And here is a poem in
praise of the tiny
green light on the
coffeepot, and the man
who each night
unfolds a filter,
measures grounds
with a wooden spoon,
adds water and comes
to bed. He likes neither
coffee nor the smell of
it, but he loves ritual,
and me, and he can't
sleep until he knows
his work is done. And I
love him. I stand in the
dark kitchen and turn
the pot on, and you'd
be surprised at the
glow a green dot
makes, how it is just
enough light to help
me find my way.

8.

Pink Floyd does
"Comfortably Numb,"
and everyone has a
lighter. This is how it's
supposed to work:
houselights go down
and we raise our
torches, sway together
beneath the flame. I
think I'll stay here
while the metal burns
my thumb and Dave
Gilmour plays a solo
you'd swear was a
woman in tears. Let's
refuse to move
forward to now, blue
lights of telephones
turning an arena cold,
so even the guitar goes
sharp and shrill. It's
best, anyway, to stay
put when the air is
burning overhead and
you find yourself an
awfully long way from
the door.

9.

Did I tell you about the
night I saw the
fireflies? It was the
first time that millions
came, sudden, so many
pinpricks in the black,
so that all I could think
was that we were fast-
sliding past planets,
cut loose. Now I know:
mating frenzy, bodies
emerging from wood, a
furious urge to glow.
That night I woke my
father, and we
watched together,
awed. Sometimes
lightning roams in
packs, pauses in
someone's woods just
long enough to terrify
—to teach us how that
kindest face looks,
pelted by light, silver
streaking down his
skin like milk.

10.

Shine a beam into the
woods at night, pan
through trees and
underbrush, and
usually you'll get what
you're after—twin
flashes of light off
retinas, and something
in the night peers back
at you, so much red
staring you down. The
woods are thick with
fear. You've seen it
glinting, just as you
once heard the
hunting scream of the
barred owl seizing its
prey. You lock the
doors but your window
is cracked to let in
breeze or breath, the
cucumber smell of the
copperhead. In your
room, you read
beneath a bulb—so
easy to pick out.

III.

Inventory

A forest can be measured in board-feet.
Somewhere right now a man
steeples his fingers beneath his chin,
looks up and presents a rough estimate:
Here are a thousand Shaker chairs,
two hundred Mission tables.

What is the world's crime
that it should be forced to pay
and pay again? I know the feeling.
Credit cards, rent, car insurance.
Just going to the mailbox
makes me numb. And then
I look around, see a clearcut
where my life ought to be.

Always leave things better
than you found them, Dad would say,
picking up spent shotgun shells
and dropping them into his pocket.
Near the end, he gave up hunting,
put a salt lick on a stump for deer
and watched them from his window.
Not that it gained him anything.
A doe still comes and licks the ground
where rain dissolved his offering.

In the bay below Pu'ukohola Heiau,
the remains of human sacrifices
were once tossed as scraps for sharks.
There I saw a single black-tipped fin
circling. Centuries after the last blood gift
she waited, expectant, ravenous.

If I might borrow some time,
I would put forth this apostrophe:
Father in heaven, there are gifts
I might have given you: a Shaker chair,
a Mission table. But I imagine
I taste you on the rim of the cup
you would drink from, and I'm not sure
how much I can afford.

Once I drove up a mountain
and was surprised by snow.
There are a thousand ways
to be unprepared, and one involves
snowmelt leaching through sneakers,
the wrong tires, everywhere timber
but no match to start a fire.
I remember I could not feel
my feet; my toes were not my own.

Filibuster

The sweaty man who taught
middle school government
made me stand each day
in the garbage can, my butt
facing the room, my nose
pressed to a chalk mark
on the board. I learned
a lot about civics that year,
and if I've never burned
a single courthouse down
it's because I'm spectacularly
unmotivated, and if
I haven't despised men
wholly, with no reason,
it's because I have a reason
and choose to swivel away,
reduced again to blond hair,
coltish legs. I start to get
the sunflower, whose every
instinct makes it stand
with its tall quorum,
who together turn
their backs on the dark.

My Mother Tells the Tristate About the Water Crisis

People don't realize,
but this is a big emergency.
Someone has sent me the link,
and there she is—my mother,
camera tight on her face.
She looks so old, lined
like an apple doll,
as she explains
how she's coped a week
without. It's gotten so bad,
she says, she's had to get water
from the ditch to flush
the commode. *That's*
how desperate people are,
the anchor says, and we all
picture her, stooped
with a bucket
at the mud bank,
having to make two
or three trips.
I'll be OK, by damn,
she tells me on the phone,
and I can see
why they chose her.
I would have picked her
myself.

For Heidi as She Heals

Be thou comforted, little dog. Thou too
in Resurrection shall have a little golden tail.

Heidi's been sick in the heart. I'm hazy
on the particulars, but there's blockage,
three arteries in a chokehold, and something
steals her oxygen, tries to slow her down.
I like Heidi—her fierceness, her profusion
of books, how she'll throw her head back
and belt out a song. She taught me to fish,
how to wade a rushing river at an angle,
just so, half fighting, half giving in. She likes
the blues, likes wildflowers, likes to think
on Luther, who asked God to let him pray
from the depths of his heart and not only
with his mouth. See, the heart matters
to a Lutheran—it's one way we have
of knowing, and it pumps like mad
as we drive our nail into whatever door
we choose. In back of Luther's hammer,
the door of that church, were relics enough
for ten cobbled-up saviors, plus Mary's milk
to feed them. Who could blame Martin
for calling out the church and all its profits?
When we met, Heidi was a roofer, a hard break
from her calling, and instead of preaching
she worked to keep out the rain. It was
a practical ministry, tuck-pointing as the sun
blazed down, but she found her way back
to the pulpit. It makes me think of those dogs
you hear about, the ones that cross a dozen states
to collapse at a door, exhausted, finally home.

God's Wife

Of course he saved
the one most delicate
for himself, and his dowry
pleased her—so much green,
so many paths for sunning.
And she is the size
of a new pencil, able to coil
her whole self
under a leaf.
He can always find her,
but keeps one eye on
the sparrow, which is to say
the rest of us. One
might see her cursive
across a rock
but nothing registers until
the tail disappears
in ferns. She writes
a poem of impeccable
beauty, a prophecy, a psalm,
but keeps his secrets
by default. They're what
she tries all day
to proclaim.

You were wrong
about the curse. No one
loves the Earth like
the serpent, each moment
the glory of embrace.
To slip inside and out again,
every muscle touching
those walls: this
is a blessing.

In the jungle are birds
whose long tails spill out
a tapestry, telling the story
of everything there is.
But here in the Ozarks, God
gave us the ring-neck:
black back, yellow collar,
a flash of orange underside
as she coils her tail
when afraid.
Do you hear what I'm saying?
When she startles
she blossoms
to flower.

Hoarder House

My childhood house is on a hill,
is full and empty. This isn't
a metaphor. I grew up there,
declared myself saved in a closet.

Mice nest in a mattress,
prom dress overtaken by moss.
I've learned not to be too attached.

If your house burns in a dream
that's the best you can hope for.
If my son wonders what
I looked like, asks for a picture,
tell him it lines a burrow.

In an empty city, trees puncture
the freeway. Buildings spill their ivy.
Only the Earth governs.
In the end, the source reclaims
both hands and artifacts.
It is possible to move freely
through the world even
if part of you is buried.

I Come to the Garden Alone

At the coffee shop today
I told a better Christian
I don't believe in heaven
or hell—feel instead a river
of intelligence courses through all things,
and we join it when we are lucky

enough to die. She took this news
about her afterlife poorly,
condemned my freeloader soul
and how it rides my body
like an old nag ambling
to a cosmic hitching post.

I saw her as I hadn't before—
as one who has not yet considered
we are paddling through otherness,
and the molecules that enter her mouth
on a gasp came from somewhere,
and maybe once were in me, in the barista—

in cave people, street preachers, nuns.
Could be she sucked off the pope's
final rattle, or even an airborne relic
of the savior's last keening—
Father, why have you forsaken us?
I feel buoyant in this brackish stream,

but my friend likes private contemplation,
a side stroll through Gethsemane,
the terrified Christ whispering comfort.
I relate more to one of the sleepers,
able, finally, to answer only to his own body,
soft snore touching the centurion's ear.

Chalkboard Mandala

In the front of the room I erase
all traces of yesterday's syntax rules,
why the comma is too weak sometimes,
news that wings past most college students,
but there, off to the left, I see flourishes
contained in a loop—little circles,
kinked tails—and I sense it means
something, that it signals urgency
and beauty. Then Rayan wants to know
how I liked his gift—my name in Arabic.
He is an artist and has wielded the chalk
sideways for softness, then turned it
to make a clean, sharp edge.
I begin to feel persuaded against
the semicolon, to see how all things
are connected by barely a breath.

Total Knee Replacement

We come to rely on the hinges—
how they lift us and let us down, soft.
Most love requires collapse.
We fold and unfold into the other,
or wrap the self in the self.
My sister has gone under knife,
a new knee where the old one
crumbled. A machine by her bed
keeps it in constant motion.
It takes training, this bending,
and so even as she sleeps
the muscles of her bicycling leg
try to remember:
this is how we rise, and how
we leave, and how we pray.

The Art of Rhetoric

Last night the cold feet of Aristotle
prodded me in the side, kept me
awake and thinking. I was working out
a new way to teach the basics
of rhetoric, and instead of sawing logos,
I tossed with the question, worried
my sheet into a toga.
I prefer small arguments,
compact ones, ones that conform
to my logic and maybe no one else's,
though I'd stake my life on most of them.
Same goes for this baby beside me,
curled against my back like the comma
my students prop so loyally between
two independent clauses, and cling to
as if they were the last contestants
in a radio contest, hands sweating
against the body of a Ford F-150 until
one by one they fall away and the semester
comes to a close. I'd like to tell them
there is nothing more convincing than
the whispered swallows I hear behind me
as my son works his bottle in his sleep.
Each nearly silent gulp makes a claim.

Speleology

I'm all for the little guy,
so I let this spider live, hang
on his filament just above
my pillow. It's a long way
to wherever he's going,
a long way back to where
he's from, composed as he is
of eight eyelashes affixed
to a speck. He is climbing,
in no hurry, and the fact
that I am awake keeps him
from spelunking
a nostril. Have you seen
those climbers who sleep
against a granite wall,
tethered in a one-man tent?
The next day they'll move on
but for the night they rest,
they wait, they put their faith
in nylon and have no use
for prayers. In this moment
everything is in abeyance,
stuck between one place
and another. They say we eat
eight spiders each year
while we sleep, so get right
with your God, spider.
As for me, I'm going in.

Walking Papers

To *get the sack* is to lose
your job. We might also say
canned, fired, given the boot.
My student has the idiom
of the day, and he takes us through
the origin of the term—how workers
would carry a bag of tools
from job to job until they were
no longer wanted, and were handed
their satchel and sent away.
My students are learning
where to put the stress, what vowels
to flatten or round, how to hear
the difference in consonants,
/p/ or /b/, /r/ or /l/, we practice,
we begin to get it right.
And this assignment shows them
there are histories we can only
guess at—that language springs
from context, purpose.
My student gets a B—enough
to keep him here, keep him
in the game. I feel for them,
those stonemasons and carvers,
painters and metalsmiths,
heading off into the unknown,
everything they own heavy
against their shoulder.

The Movement You Need

The key, you know, is emphasis. English
is a stress-toned language, and we listen
for the punch, in a word, in a sentence,
and that extra *oomph*, that little flex,
is all we need to make sense of a thing.
There is an exercise for this—to convey
that where we stretch a syllable matters,
gives resonance, expression, and that's
why I am singing, my voice meeting
those of my students, visitors here,
people who have been misunderstood
by cashiers and taxi drivers,
the lilting mismatch of Arabic, Polish,
Yoruba, Japanese, but today in class
we layer vowel over vowel, and we sing,
no hesitation, all voices present and clear
from the first "Hey, Jude." I tell them
they can swallow most of a word,
but if they nail the stress, we'll get them,
we'll know where they come from.
When I was a child, I watched
the black record turn, green Apple
rolling over and over, and I knew
every word, and I sang them all,
and I tried to understand—*the movement
you need is on your shoulder*, what
did that mean? Even Paul thought it
a bit of nonsense, and he planned
to revise, but John said that was the best
line in the song, and it's in there still,
and we sing it together, and it means
something, some fluttering by the ear,
apple rolling, rolling down a hill.
Don't you know that it's just you,

hey Jude, you'll do, and we do know,
we feel it, we punch each key word
to drive it home, into our heart,
then we can start to make it better.

Note

Humansville is a southwest Missouri town of just over a thousand people. It was named after an early settler, James Human.

Thank You

My parents shared a core belief, and it's one I heard regularly when I was growing up: Anything you read is good for you. I'd test them on this—cereal boxes, Dr. Seuss, porn? Yes, they insisted; you could learn a lot from all of that, but everything is best in its own good time. Thank you, Donald and Elsie Craigo, for making a wordsmith of me.

I have the best press in the world, and the kindest, in Sundress Publications, with its brilliant editor, Erin Elizabeth Smith. Thank you, Erin, for making a real poet of me.

And my family gives me something to look forward to every day, as well as a reason to work hard and to try to be my very best self. Thank you, loved ones, for making a fairly good human of me.

About the Author

Karen Craigo is the editor and general manager of *The Marshfield Mail*, a weekly newspaper in southwestern Missouri. Her first collection, *No More Milk*, was published by Sundress in 2016, and she is also the author of two chapbooks: *Someone Could Build Something Here* (Winged City, 2013) and *Stone for an Eye* (Kent State/Wick, 2004). Her poetry, fiction, essays, and journalism are widely published, and she maintains *Better View of the Moon*, a blog on writing, editing, and creativity. She is the nonfiction editor and former editor-in-chief of *Mid-American Review* and the interviews editor of *SmokeLong Quarterly*.

Other Sundress Titles

Match Cut
Letitia Trent
$16

Phantom Tongue
Steven Sanchez
$15

Citizens of the Mausoleum
Rodney Gomez
$15

Either Way, You're Done
Stephanie McCarley Dugger
$15

Before Isadore
Shannon Elizabeth Hardwick
$15

Big Thicket Blues
Natalie Giarratano
$15

At Whatever Front
Les Kay
$15

No More Milk
Karen Craigo
$15

Theater of Parts
M. Mack
$15

Divining Bones
Charlie Bondus
$16

The Minor Territories
Danielle Sellers
$15

Actual Miles
Jim Warner
$15

Hands That Break and Scar
Sarah A. Chavez
$15

They Were Bears
Sarah Marcus
$15

Babbage's Dream
Neil Aitken
$15

Posada
Xochitl Julisa Bermejo
$15

Suites for the Modern Dancer
Jill Khoury
$15

What Will Keep Us Alive
Kristin LaTour
$15